A Play by Bob Hescott

```
BUXTON
SUPPORT CENTRE
1 8 MAY 2005
RECEIVED
```

Series Editors: Steve Barlow and Steve Skidmore

Heinemann Educational Publishers
Halley Court, Jordan Hill, Oxford OX2 8EJ
Part of Harcourt Education

Heinemann is the registered trademark of
Harcourt Education Limited

© Bob Hescott, 2003

First published 2003

07 06 05 04 03
10 9 8 7 6 5 4 3 2 1

British Library Cataloguing in Publication Data is available
from the British Library on request.

ISBN 0 435 21378 4

Copyright notice

All rights reserved. No part of this publication may be reproduced in any form or by any means (including photocopying or storing it in any medium by electronic means and whether or not transiently or incidentally to some other use of this publication) without the written permission of the copyright owner, except in accordance with the provisions of the Copyright, Designs and Patents Act 1988 or under the terms of a licence issued by the Copyright Licensing Agency, 90 Tottenham Court Road, London W1T 4LP. Applications for the copyright owner's written permission should be addressed to the publisher.

Illustrations by Peter Wilks
Cover illustrated by Geo Parkin
Cover design by Shireen Nathoo Design
Designed and typeset by Artistix, Thame, Oxon
Printed and bound in Great Britain by Biddles Ltd

Original illustrations © Harcourt Education Limited, 2002

Tel: 01865 888058 www.heinemann.co.uk

Contents

Characters   4

Scene 1   The cast of *Faberoony* assemble in the studio   7

Scene 2   Magnus and Ahsen discover something interesting about Keith   16

Scene 3   A goddess appears on *Faberoony*   25

Staging instructions

When Sarah speaks in her microphone to Ahsen, only he can hear her in his headphones. To signal this to the audience, he cups his hand around one headphone and looks towards Sarah. The rest of the cast shouldn't react at all.

Characters

Ed is the talent that holds together the live Saturday morning kids' show *Faberoony*. But when his girlfriend Trudy dumps him, his world falls apart, and so does *Faberoony*.

Gail is vain and less talented than she believes. She's always watching for things to go wrong, so she can save the show.

Ron is the running gag of the show. Each week he appears in a different over-the-top costume.

Trudy has the looks of a goddess and has won the heart of Ed.

Magnus is a macho type who made his name upsetting wild animals.

Sarah, the producer of *Faberoony* is building up to her nineteenth nervous breakdown.

Ahsen is the floor manager in contact with the producer in the gallery via headphones.

Scene One

A TV studio. Ahsen is receiving a message in his headphones from Sarah in the control gallery. Ed and Gail are both checking the script.

ED: Ahsen! Ahsen!

AHSEN: What's up, Ed?

ED: Let me see the menu for today's show again.

AHSEN: Right.

GAIL: Not learnt it yet, Ed?

ED: No.

GAIL: Don't worry. If you dry, I'll do it. I've got a first-rate memory.

ED: In your dreams, Gail.

(Ahsen hands Ed his clipboard.)

AHSEN: Here's the menu.

ED: Cheers. *(Reads from clipboard)* And we've got a great line-up for this morning's show. First up, cartoon fun with *Cat and the Canary*. Then it's icky-sticky time with Ron!

(Ron enters with a leap. He is dressed as a dog.)

RON: You called? Woof! Woof! Woof!

ED: *(Handing the menu back to Ahsen)* Right. I know the menu from this point.

RON: Who am I splatting this week?

GAIL: Kid sisters.

AHSEN: With cold curry in a sock.

ED: It says here it's cold custard.

AHSEN: My mum doesn't do custard.

SARAH: *(Into her mike)* Ahsen?

AHSEN: *(Into his mike)* Yes, Sarah?

SARAH: Have you collected up the mobile phones yet?

AHSEN: Doing it now, boss. Mobile phones, everyone! Come on, Sarah says hand them over.

RON: It's in here somewhere.

GAIL: Here.

AHSEN: Thanks.

RON: Ah, the old dog and bone. Woof! Woof!

AHSEN: Down, boy! *(To Ed)* Can I have your phone?

ED: There you go.

(As Ed hands over his phone, it rings. He takes the call.)

ED: Ed here. Oh hi, Trudy, thinking of you. How's the sunshine of my life? What? What? What! Hang on! She's rung off.

GAIL: Something up, Ed?

ED: The dumb, stupid dimwit! She's dumped me!

AHSEN: Why?

ED: She said I didn't respect her.

GAIL: But you said she was the love of your life.

ED: She was.

GAIL: You must feel really bad.

ED: I do.

GAIL: Don't worry. I'll carry you if you start to lose it.

AHSEN: Oh no.

RON: *(Anxiously)* Woof woof.

SARAH: Ahsen, where's Magnus the beastman?

AHSEN: With Keith.

SARAH: Who's Keith?

AHSEN: This week's animal guest. A kangaroo. The oldest kangaroo in the world.

RON: Keith is a really great roo. I love him. He's an old friend.

SARAH: Right, starting places. Gee them up, Ahsen. I'm starting the countdown.

AHSEN: Starting places, everyone. Quiet on the floor! Ron, you're off, and Magnus, keep that kangaroo quiet!

(Magnus appears.)

MAGNUS: Kangaroos don't make a noise.

AHSEN: Then you shut up.

(Magnus disappears again.)

SARAH: Counting down then, nine, eight, seven …

(Ed and Gail go into welcoming smiles.)

AHSEN: … six, five, four, three …

ED: *(Suddenly stops smiling)* I can't do this. *(He exits)*

AHSEN: … two, one. We're live!

GAIL: *(Gawping helplessly)* Right, yes … Faberoony! Yes, that's it, Faberoony! We've got a great show for you this afternoon.

SARAH: This morning!

GAIL: First off, cartoon fun with *Dog and the Parrot*!

(We hear the cartoon start with loud music. The cast relax as they are off air.)

SARAH: It's *Cat and the Canary*! Ahsen, where's Ed? Find him! Gail will sink us with her mouth.

GAIL: How did I do?

AHSEN: Sarah says you were great. Where's Ed?

(Ron appears, carrying two plates of bananas and jam.)

RON: He's in the loo, crying.

AHSEN: I'll speak to him during the icky-sticky spot.

RON: Now remember, Gail. You mustn't tell the kids they can't use their hands to eat the bananas and jam until they've come up.

GAIL: Right.

SARAH: Stand them by, Ahsen.

AHSEN: On your marks, please. Stand by, studio. And – action!

GAIL: Right, folks, it's Icky-Sticky Time!

RON: Woof! Woof! Woof!

GAIL: Ron says who likes bananas? *(Cheers from audience)* Great!

RON: Woof! Woof! Woof!

GAIL: And who likes jam? *(Cheers from audience)* Great!

RON: Woof! Woof ! Woof!

GAIL: And Ron says, who thinks they can eat a plate of jam and bananas fastest … *(Cheers from audience)* … without using their hands?

(Sudden silence from audience.)

RON: Aargh!!!

SARAH: Stupid girl! They've all put their hands down again.

GAIL: Oh – come on. We need just two people to come forward to have some sticky fun. What about you at the back? – oh.

RON: Woof! Woof! Gail, do you like bananas?

GAIL: Oh yes, I love them!

RON: And do you like jam?

GAIL: I adore jam.

RON: That's good, because you can have them.

(Ron splats Gail with the two plates of jam and bananas, one on each cheek. Gail screams in dismay.)

RON: Woof! Woof! Time for a break!

GAIL: *(Miserably)* But when we come back we've got Len, the world's oldest badger.

SARAH: It's a kangaroo called Keith! I'll swing for her, stupid girl!

Scene Two

The TV studio, after the break.

16

GAIL: I'm all sticky!

AHSEN: Here's a damp cloth, Gail. Clean yourself up before the adverts end.

(Gail starts to wipe off the jam and bananas. The sound of a wasp buzzing is heard.)

GAIL: Thanks. Yuk! I bet I get a rash. The things I do for fame. What's that noise?

AHSEN: What?

GAIL: I thought so, a wasp. It's after the jam.

RON: You got it off just in time, then.

GAIL: No thanks to you.

SARAH: Ahsen, what's the news on Ed?

AHSEN: I've made him a cup of tea. He's talking about doing the Jolly Joke spot.

SARAH: Right. And make Gail go through the kid sister splat stuff with Ron. She's hopeless.

AHSEN: Right, boss. *(To Gail)* Sarah says you're doing great. She just wants you to brush up on the splat stuff.

GAIL: Okay. Right, folks, time to splat a kid sister, and this week any kid sisters who can't answer three simple questions, will be splatted with a stick of rock!!

RON: No! Custard.

GAIL: Stick of custard.

AHSEN: No! Curry.

GAIL: Stick of curry.

RON: No! Sock.

GAIL: Sock of rock!

SARAH: I'll swing for her!

AHSEN: Sarah says you're doing really well. Places, everyone – and we're live.

RON: Woof! Woof! Welcome back to *Faberoony*!

GAIL: Now it's time for Jolly Jokes.

(Ed enters.)

ED: Hi, folks, I'm back.

(Although Ed says the words, being sad has made him slow and dreamy.)

GAIL: Hi, Ed!

ED: Bye Gail.

(Gail exits.)

RON: Woof! Woof! Here's a jolly joke. I said here's a jolly joke.

ED: *(Trying hard to be happy)* Let's have it then, Ron.

RON: My dog has no nose.

ED: What?

RON: I said, my dog has no nose.

ED: *(Sadly)* I'm really sorry about that, Ron. That's really sad.

GAIL: *(Offstage)* How does he smell?

ED: What? *(He sniffs Ron)* A bit sweaty – the usual.

RON: My wife's gone to the West Indies!

ED: Without you? I know what that feels like. My Trudy's dumped me.

GAIL: *(Offstage)* Jamaica?

ED: Did I make her? I suppose I did. Yes, I suppose I made her dump me. I didn't value her. I took her for granted.

RON: Time for a cartoon!

ED: Is it? I was enjoying our chat. I was telling you about Trudy. How I miss her, how I'm sad.

RON: Woof! Woof! Faberoony!!!

ED: Not really. It's all right to be sad, kids. Life isn't always faberoony. I'm sad today. I've lost someone I really liked. Being sad is okay, if that's how you feel.

(Gail enters.)

GAIL: But this cartoon will cheer us up, Ed. It's the one about the fastest mouse in all Belgium!

(Sound of cartoon starting.)

AHSEN: Right. We're off air for a minute.

ED: I thought that went well.

RON: Well? You killed all my gags, man!

GAIL: Lucky I was there.

SARAH: Ahsen, get Ed off the floor. He's lost it.

AHSEN: Right. Ed, sorry, show's over.

ED: Really? It seems shorter this week.

AHSEN: Let's get you to your dressing room. You can lie down there.

ED: Right.

(Ed exits as Magnus enters.)

MAGNUS: Bit wet, this kangaroo, don't you think?

AHSEN: I'm sorry?

MAGNUS: I mean, the kids have seen me fight a croc and a snake and a bear. This is a bit dull, don't you think? An old kangaroo?

AHSEN: No. The kids hate you fighting the animals.

MAGNUS: Well, I hate kids. They're all wimps. Couldn't we give the kangaroo some boxing gloves and I could punch it about a bit?

RON: If he punches Keith, I'm going to punch him. I love that roo.

AHSEN: Leave it out, Magnus. Off you go, Ron, see if Ed's all right.

(Ron exits.)

MAGNUS: Right. I'd better get ready. *(He looks into the animal crate)* Now that's interesting.

AHSEN: What is?

MAGNUS: Keith's the oldest kangaroo in the world, isn't he?

AHSEN: Yes.

MAGNUS: Well he isn't any more.

AHSEN: Isn't he?

MAGNUS: No. He's dead.

SARAH: Get set, cartoon's ending, everything okay on the floor, Ahsen?

AHSEN: No, the kangaroo's dead!

SARAH: What?!

AHSEN: It was very old, and now it isn't. It's history! What do we do?

SARAH: Quick! Tie it up. Make it seem alive. Wiggle it around. I'll tell the cameras to stay on Magnus.

AHSEN: Tie it to what?

SARAH: Anything! Tie it to a mike stand! Quick!

AHSEN: Where's Ron?

MAGNUS: You sent him to Ed's dressing room.

AHSEN: I know I'm going to regret this but – Gail!

GAIL: Yes.

AHSEN: You'll have to cover while I string up the late kangaroo.

GAIL: At last! My chance.

SARAH: Stand by, studio. We're going live again!

Scene Three

The TV studio. Ahsen has finished tying the kangaroo to a mike stand. He gives a thumbs-up to Magnus and lifts the pole so that the kangaroo appears to be standing.

25

GAIL: Welcome back! Wasn't that great, kids? Now it's time to meet the beastman!

MAGNUS: Hi, Gail, I've got a very old friend here. Why don't you come and meet him?

GAIL: So let's go over to Magnus and Keith, the oldest thingy in the world.

(Magnus is standing in front of Keith. Ahsen is holding up the mike stand to which Keith is attached.)

MAGNUS: Good day, one and all. I'm Magnus the Beast Man. You might remember me from when I fought the croc.

(The wasp sound is growing louder.)

MAGNUS: Today it's all a bit tamer. Meet Keith, the oldest kangaroo in the world.

(Magnus steps to one side to reveal Keith very briefly before stepping back in front of him.)

MAGNUS: But to get back to me. I'm not afraid of any animal. I'll fight snakes, tigers, bears – what's that?

GAIL: I think it's a wasp. It's after that spilled jam.

MAGNUS: A wasp? Make it go away! I hate bugs! Shoo! Shove off! Help!

(Magnus starts to wave his arms wildly.)

SARAH: Get the camera off him!

MAGNUS: Someone save me! Aargh!!! I've been stung!

GAIL: Er – er – let me tell you everything I know about kangaroos.

SARAH: Good girl! Get the mike over to her, Ahsen!

GAIL: Kangaroos can hop, and they have a pouch.

(Ahsen swings the mike stand. Keith is still tied to it. As the mike arrives over Gail's head, Keith's body smacks into her head and knocks her out.)

GAIL: I hear birdies. *(She falls to the floor)*

SARAH: Magnus! Someone! Do something!

(Magnus is sitting on the floor. He holds up his thumb.)

MAGNUS: Thumb. Hurt.

(Ron enters.)

RON: Never fear, Ron's here!

(Ron does a take on Keith.)

RON: What's this? Keith dead? Keith the kangaroo, the person Ron most loved, is no more? *(He starts to blub loudly)* Dead! He's dead! Dead and never called me Ron!

SARAH: Ahsen! You'll have to do something!

AHSEN: Not me.

SARAH: We're going out live, this is killing us. Ahsen!

(Ahsen lays down the mike stand. He passes the whimpering Magnus, the unconscious Gail and the blubbing Ron. He approaches the audience, fearfully.)

AHSEN: Fab – fab – faberoony! Everyone having a good time? *(Silence)* Good. Let's have some fun. Did you know fun was invented by the Greeks?

SARAH: No!

AHSEN: The Greeks believed the gods and goddesses could come down to earth, and help out people in trouble. Help!

(Trudy walks onto the set.)

TRUDY: Yes? What's up?

AHSEN: Who are you, mystery guest?

TRUDY: I'm Trudy.

ED: *(Offstage)* Trudy?

TRUDY: Ed?

(Ed appears.)

ED: Is that really you, Trudy?

TRUDY: Is that really you, Ed?

AHSEN: Is this really me? – I think so.

TRUDY: I've been watching the show. I heard what you said about being sad. You really care about me, don't you?

ED: With all my heart.

TRUDY: Ed?

ED: Yes, Trudy?

TRUDY: You're not dumped any more.

AHSEN: Live on television, folks! Hearts mended. Lives repaired.

ED: Oh Trudy!

TRUDY: Oh Ed!

MAGNUS: *(Clutching his thumb)* Oh mummy, it hurts!

RON: *(Wailing and banging his head on the floor)* Dead! Dead!

GAIL: *(Semi-conscious)* Dog and the Badger!

SARAH: Take us into a cartoon. Wind up the scene!

AHSEN: Over to you, Ed.

ED: This is Ed, happy Ed, wishing you a happy life. After the cartoon, we're picking on little sisters.

TRUDY: Wow! I know I hate mine.

ED: Then more cartoon fun, and Ron will be back as a duck.

RON: Quack quack.

GAIL: *(Trying to get up and join in)* It was a kangaroo. It flew! I'm sure of it. *(She falls back into unconsciousness)*

ED: And please kids, don't let off fireworks in your hands.

TRUDY: No.

ED: Get your grandad to hold them!

TRUDY: Bye for now.

RON: Woof woof. It's *Cat and the Canary* time!

ALL: Faberoony!

(Blackout.)